# GLOBAL INDUSTRIES
## UNCOVERED
# THE TOURISM INDUSTRY

## RICHARD SPILSBURY

WAYLAND

Published in 2012 by Wayland

Copyright © Wayland 2012

Wayland
338 Euston Road
London NW1 3BH

Wayland Australia
Level 17/207 Kent Street
Sydney NSW 2000

Series Editor: Claire Shanahan
Editor: Susie Brooks
Design: Rebecca Painter
Picture Researcher: Shelley Noronha

British Library Cataloguing in Publication Data

Spilsbury, Richard, 1963-
   The tourism industry. -- (Global industries uncovered)
   1. Tourism--Juvenile literature.
   2. Industrial location--Juvenile literature.
   3. Globalization--Economic aspects--Juvenile literature.
   I. Title II. Series
   338.4'791-dc22

ISBN 978 0 7502 6946 9

Picture acknowledgments: Cover and 11 KPA/Zuma/Rex
Features; 7 © Eye Ubiquitous/Corbis; 8, 39 © Encompass
Graphics Ltd; 10 © Chris Martin Bahr/Rex Features; 12 ©
JASON REED/Reuters/Corbis; 13, 15 Getty Images; 17 © Tony
Roberts/CORBIS; 18 David Madison/Getty Images; 19
www.CartoonStock.com; 20 ©Rex Features; 22 © Roy
Garner/Rex Features; 25 AFP/Getty Images; 27 ©Thomas Cook
Ltd; 28 © Grootbos Private Nature Reserve; 29 Sally de Jager,
BEN Bicycle Tourism Director; 31 ©Grootbos Private Nature
Reserve; 34 © James Leynse/Corbis; 35 © Jose Fuste
Raga/Corbis; 36 © John Gollings/Arcaid/Corbis; 38 © Jan
Rihak/Istock; 40 © John Van Hasselt/CORBIS SYGMA; 41 ©
Catherine Karnow/CORBIS

Printed in China

Wayland is a division of Hachette Children's Books,
an Hachette UK company.
www.hachette.co.uk

# Contents

*Matt is 14 and has just returned from a scout trip to Nepal. The scout group booked the trip through a trekking company based in the UK, bought trekking gear made in China, flew with a Middle Eastern airline and stayed in a hotel owned by a US hotel group. They went sightseeing to an ancient city reconstructed and maintained using German money, and mountain biking on US bikes. Matt is just one of billions of tourists worldwide and his trip was part of the global tourism industry.*

## The holiday industry

Tourism is a major global industry linking tourists and the diverse places to which they want to travel. It is a composite industry, which means it is made up of and served by lots of different, interconnected industries. Before a holiday begins, many tourists use travel agents and tour operators to book their trip, insurance companies for financial protection, clothes shops to buy their holiday outfits, and book shops and publishers to find their reading material. Tourists then make use of the transport industry to get to their destinations, the hotel industry to find a place to stay, and the restaurant and retail industries to provide meals.

This is a simple representation of some of the interconnected parts of the tourism industry.

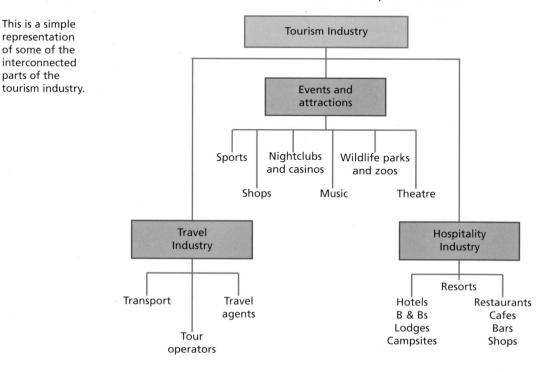

6

## How tourism went global

In 1950, there were around 25 million tourists worldwide, but by the year 2000 this had risen to 700 million. There have been many changes over the last 50 years or so that have allowed the rapid expansion and globalisation of the tourism industry. These include transport innovations such as quicker, larger jet aeroplanes like Boeing 747s. These aircraft can carry up to 490 passengers on non-stop 17-hour trips, covering over 12,000 kilometres. The price of travel has dropped partly as a consequence of fitting more passengers on each plane, and partly because of the development of 'one-size-fits-all' package holidays. These are trips organised by a tour operator to include travel, accommodation and usually food. Package holidays provide a near-identical holiday experience for many individuals.

The increasingly widespread use of the internet for marketing and booking holidays is another important development. People can now search travel schedules and book holidays directly from home – something that was impossible just a few decades ago. However, the technological revolutions that have aided the spread of the tourism industry are not equally accessible globally, owing to differences in wealth, which is why people in more developed countries (MDCs) make up the majority of international tourists.

Technology has increased opportunities for tourism in many places. These tourists are taking part in a tour of Paris using Segway transporters.

## Scales of tourism

Tourism is an immense industry. In 2011, there were almost 1 billion international tourist arrivals at airports, ferry ports and border crossings around the world, and globally tourists spent over US$900 billion on their holidays. One in every twelve people in the global workforce is employed directly or indirectly by tourism. Tourist businesses vary widely, from numerous one-person industries, such as souvenir stalls, to businesses with a few branches each employing several people, such as national travel agents, to a few very large enterprises, such as the international hotel chain Best Western. Best Western operates over 4,000 hotels in 80 countries. Some tourism companies, such as a surf school, occupy only a small space, but others are giant resorts covering many square kilometres of land.

Tourism also has a global impact by connecting different people around the world. Such connections can stimulate positive intermingling of cultures, spread knowledge, and act as a focus for community and national development. For example, since China opened up to Western tourists in 1978 after decades of political and cultural isolation, democracy and individual freedom have gradually increased in China and knowledge of Chinese culture has grown in the West.

## Location, location

Tourists can now visit virtually any place on Earth – even extreme habitats such as Death Valley, USA, or Antarctica. People may travel to particular places to see natural features, such as tropical rainforests or coral reefs, or human attractions including unique buildings, festivals and city shops. Different regions may also develop their own general specialisms, such as winter sports in the Alps, safaris in Africa, stately homes in the UK, and beach or cruise holidays in the Caribbean. Some locations attract visitors for unusual reasons. Adventure tourists may visit a remote, deep valley simply to seek thrills such as rope jumping and medical tourists may seek out locations where they can have operations that would be too expensive or unavailable elsewhere.

Winter sports resorts dominate the tourism industry in the European Alps.

**Alpine Skiing**
- Major ski resort

GERMANY

AUSTRIA

FRANCE

LICHTENSTEIN St Anton

Kitzbuhel  Saalbach  Schladming

Mayrhofen

SWITZERLAND  Obergurgl  Neustift

Grindelwald  Arosa  Davos  Alta  Almdorf

Andermatt  Badia  Nassfeld

Avoriaz  Whitepod  St Moritz  Bormio  Cortina

La Clusaz  Verbier  Zermatt

Chamonix  Champoluc  ITALY  SLOVENIA

Tignes

Les Trois Vallées  Val D'Isere

Alpe D'Huez  Sauze

Serre Chevalier  d'Oulx

0   50  100 km

0       50      100 miles

> *What an odd thing tourism is. You fly off to a strange land… and then expend vast quantities of time and money in a largely futile attempt to recapture the comforts that you wouldn't have lost if you hadn't left home in the first place.*
>
> Bill Bryson, author, 1991

Tourism has varying importance for different places. In India tourism is widespread, from the deserts of Rajasthan to the temples of Delhi, yet its contribution to GDP (total value of goods and services) is dwarfed by that of other industries including IT, steel and textiles. Over 75 per cent of the GDP of nearby Maldives, a group of tropical islands, comes from tourism. Since 1990, increases in tourism to boost GDP have raised the share of the global tourist trade in LDCs by over 9 per cent each year.

## SPOTLIGHT

### Big players

Some of the biggest players in the tourism industry are transnational corporations (TNCs). These often have their headquarters in one country but may have bases and produce goods or offer services in several others. They include global airlines, such as British Airways, and more varied companies such as the German tourism group TUI AG that runs a range of mostly European travel companies. Some important tourism companies are themselves one part of a portfolio of businesses owned by large, diverse TNCs. For example, Virgin group includes publishers, music stores, mobile networks and health clubs alongside train and airline companies.

Global travel companies such as TUI AG can manage and optimise their profits from each stage in a holiday, from booking to transport to hotels.

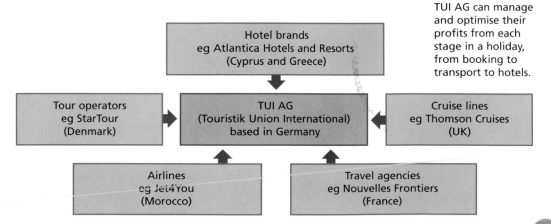

Hotel brands
eg Atlantica Hotels and Resorts
(Cyprus and Greece)

Tour operators
eg StarTour
(Denmark)

TUI AG
(Touristik Union International)
based in Germany

Cruise lines
eg Thomson Cruises
(UK)

Airlines
eg Jet4You
(Morocco)

Travel agencies
eg Nouvelles Frontiers
(France)

# Global dimensions of tourism

The businesses making up the tourism industry do not exist in isolation. They are interdependent with other industries, the environment and societies – on local, national and international scales. Tourism has both positive and negative impacts on people and places around the world.

## Outside the tourism industry

Tourism is closely interlinked with many other industries, including farming and food preparation. These industries grow and supply the ingredients, snacks and meals for sale in cafes, restaurants, hotels and shops. Sometimes they are located near the tourist industries, but in many TNC hotels in LDCs, food is brought in from MDC countries where many guests come from, in order to supply them with familiar meals. When fewer tourists stay in a region, these industries may face a downturn. At the same time, successes in other industries can enhance tourism, for example football fans may travel to different countries to support their teams if they progress further in competitions.

Some shopkeepers sell mostly souvenirs made for tourists, such as these carved animal horns. When tourists stay away, local livelihoods may be threatened.

## Changes on the inside

Different businesses and locations within the tourism industry are also globally interdependent. Holiday destination choices can change for many reasons, leaving people in the industry out of work in one area. For example, UK travel companies marketed holidays in the Costa del Sol, Spain, in the 1970s, but by the 1990s other low-cost sunny destinations such as Gambia in West Africa were being promoted, and tourist revenue in Spain dropped. The reasons were largely economic as cheaper airfares to Africa, and lower local wages, allowed the companies to make a bigger profit. When a destination dominated by hotels and holiday services owned by TNCs loses popularity, TNCs may just close down and shift resources to a more popular location, leaving local employees out of work.

## The spread of tourism

The tourism industry forms a network linking different parts of the world. This network has developed and spread partly as a result of infrastructure, so out of two similar possible holiday destinations, the one with easiest access to major transport hubs may develop more quickly. The network is sometimes interrelated with what happened in the distant past. For example, Jamaica was a British colony up until the 19th century and many Jamaicans moved to the UK in the 1950s to work in British industries. Today, many UK citizens who have links with Jamaica choose to go there on holiday, often to visit relatives and friends. Tourism links between countries are also related to proximity, as people tend to have holidays close to home because they are cheaper than travelling longer distances. Thus, more visitors to Mexico are from the USA than from Europe.

The tourism industry has not only spread geographically, but has also stratified into different levels within locations. For example, tourism businesses may offer holidays at a variety of different price bands in the same place. There may be more basic, cheap accommodation for backpackers and luxury hotels for richer travellers, or family- and student-orientated attractions all close to the same tourist destination. This stratification allows companies to ensure they bring in money, whatever the tourists' interest or budget.

Camel rides are part of the generic desert experience offered by tour operators not only in the Middle East, as here in Petra, Jordan, but also in India and Australia!

## SPOTLIGHT

### Generic holidays

Global tour operators often market holidays by type rather than by individual places. For example, they offer a range of winter sun, summer sun, or ski breaks. Holidaymakers may then select their holiday by comparing prices and facilities for a generic holiday. For example, a UK visitor may choose a winter sun break in Egypt as it is cheaper than going to Barbados. The individuality of the actual location is less important for many tourists. In the case of globalised chains of resorts or hotels, facilities such as the layout of rooms are standard all over the world.

## Physical processes and tourism

Changes in tourism are closely interconnected with physical geographical processes. For instance, wave action is washing away Hawaii's famous Waikiki beach, and a 2008 Hawaii Tourism Authority report warned of the loss of thousands of tourism jobs and revenue of nearly US$2 billion each year as a result. Major destructive events such as volcanic eruptions, earthquakes and hurricanes have a sudden, spectacular effect on tourism. Hurricane Wilma devastated the Mexican tourist region of the Yucatan peninsula in 2005, causing a drop in tourist income of £1.3 billion in 2006.

Hurricane Katrina devastated the city of New Orleans, transforming the normally busy tourist district into a waterlogged ghost town.

Physical processes can also increase the numbers of tourists. For example, heavy snowfall in mountain areas attracts skiers to ski resorts and sunny spells draw crowds to beaches. Crowds of people also visit particular locations to witness periodic or unusual events. In Japan, there are annual flower-viewing parties when people come to places such as Okayama to see the widespread cherry blossom, or Sakura, in spring. Tourism increased in Cornwall, UK, in 1999 and in Libya in 2006 as these locations were good for viewing total solar eclipses.

## SPOTLIGHT

### Airlines and the oil industry

Between 2006 and the middle of 2008, global oil prices almost tripled, owing in part to a shortage of oil in the Middle East and other countries. Some airlines, such as XL, went bust, and others struggled to make profits because their fuel costs rose. One effect of airline failure on tourists was surging travel costs as surviving tourism companies tried to cover the increased costs. For example, the cost of a week in Corfu from the UK with Olympic Holidays cost £200 the day before XL failed, and £352 the day after. The oil price dropped again at the end of 2008, but airlines continued to struggle as global banking problems meant fewer people could afford to travel.

## Human processes and tourism

People's actions can also have positive and negative influences on tourism. Human processes that increase tourism include the restoration of ancient buildings, such as the ancient town of Lijiang, China, and the development of infrastructure to improve access for tourists, such as the suspended walkway over the Grand Canyon, USA. Changing political situations may help or hinder tourism, too. For example, the change in Nepalese rule from a royal family to a more democratic political party in 2007 increased tourism, but political unrest and violence in Kenya in early 2007 caused a 78 per cent drop in tourist numbers.

XL airlines invested its money in offering cheap flights and had little saved up in case fuel prices increased. In 2008, they ran out of money to buy fuel, leaving their passengers stranded at airports.

The biggest negative effect on tourism caused by human processes in the early 21st century was terrorism. The ripple effect of the 9/11 attacks on New York and Washington, D.C. shrank US arrivals by around 6 million in 2002 compared with 2001. The bombing of tourist resorts also severely affected tourism in Bali and Sharm-El-Sheik, Egypt. Other human actions that can impact on tourism in one place include intentionally started forest fires and the vandalism and removal of antiquities, as has happened at the famous Angkor Wat temple in Cambodia.

## Who pays for tourism?

Tourists bring wealth to economies not only because they stimulate jobs in tourism, but also because they may pay using foreign currencies, which are often more stable in value than local currencies. At Malé airport, the Maldives, Western tourists pay in dollars and receive Maldivian currency as change. When governments of LDCs and poorer regions in MDCs want to attract more tourists, they often have to improve facilities for tourists as well as local infrastructure, such as good roads. Many LDCs borrow money for development from international banks and organisations such as the International Monetary Fund (IMF) and the World Bank, but sometimes development is paid for by private companies. Some tourist destinations also help to pay for tourism infrastructure using taxes charged, for example, at airports or on arrival in particular areas.

A problem with development for tourists is that it sometimes excludes local people. For example, poor people may not be able to afford goods and services in new shopping malls, restaurants, tourist hospitals and sports centres. What is more, only an estimated 10–15 per cent of money spent by tourists actually reaches the residents and businesses in tourist centres. The rest of the tourist money often 'leaks' from the area to businesses such as tour companies based elsewhere.

## SPOTLIGHT

### Attracting tourists

Governments often create international advertising campaigns to attract tourists to their countries. These can be very popular. For example, Tourism New Zealand responded to global interest in the *Lord of the Rings* trilogy of films by advertising the fact that they were shot in locations across the islands. This stimulated a 34 per cent increase in visitor numbers during the cinema releases of the films, and today trips to see 'Mount Doom' (Tongariro National Park) and other trilogy sites are still very popular.

Other campaigns are flops. Tourism Australia spent AUS$180 million in 2006 on major ads with the line, 'So where the bloody hell are you?' This caused controversy in countries such as Singapore, Canada and the UK, when people complained about the wording, and failed to attract visitors. In fact, numbers of tourists dropped from the previous year. Tourism Australia hoped that its campaign tied in with the 2008 blockbuster film *Australia* would prove to be more successful.

## Keeping an eye on tourism

The groups responsible for governing and regulating tourism vary in scale. They include local civil society groups, such as religious organisations, groups of powerful businesspeople, government departments and global institutions. For example, the International Air Transport Association (IATA) represents 230 airlines and regulates aspects of air travel such as safety, air pollution and prices. Groups regulating tourism also include charities such as Tourism Concern. This organisation, based in the UK, fights exploitation of people, such as poor working conditions for tourist hotel staff or increases in sex tourism. The charity publicises problems and encourages responsible and fair treatment of people by putting pressure on, or lobbying against, parts of the tourism industry.

The problem with shared governance is that different groups have different visions of the goals for tourism. For example, governments may promote the development of the tourist industry in a mountain range to create jobs for many people, but potential tourists to the mountain range may oppose any development in the area as it may spoil the scenery they hope to enjoy on their future holidays.

In 2008, Tourism Australia's hopes for boosting tourism revenue were tied in with the release of the film *Australia*, which featured a largely Australian cast including Nicole Kidman and Hugh Jackman (above), and celebrated the sweeping landscapes of the country itself.

## Tourists and the environment

The spread and development of the tourism industry has varied impacts on the physical world. The most significant globally is the contribution of tourist travel to global warming. About one-fifth of the total distance of all tourist travel is by air, and aircraft contribute far more to global warming per kilometre travelled than any other form of transport. All engines that burn oil-based fuels release carbon dioxide into the atmosphere, which traps heat, adding to the greenhouse effect. However, aircraft engines emit greenhouse gases high in the sky, where a stronger warming effect persists longer than at lower levels.

Global warming is causing changes in sea level, rainfall patterns and extreme weather events, affecting agriculture and many other industries including tourism itself. For example, sea-level rise in the Maldives may eventually submerge these low-lying tropical islands, which are highly dependent on tourist income.

There are many more environmental impacts of tourism, including pollution of the oceans by cruise ships, and the destruction of rare reef ecosystems by runoff of pollution from coastal resorts and irresponsible harvest of coral by and for holidaymakers. Trips offering close encounters with endangered gorillas or chimps may expose the great apes to diarrhoea, coughs and throat infections against which they have little immunity. However, the presence of tourists can also greatly improve environments. For example, some tourists take holidays in which they contribute to studies of endangered species, such as black rhinos, that aid in that species' conservation. Payments by tourists to visit national parks, reserves and other biodiverse places contribute towards wages for wardens who protect the areas from illegal deforestation and hunting.

## The sustainable alternative

The tourism industry is putting increasing efforts into being sustainable in order to benefit the natural and social environments of tourist areas now and into the future. The United Nations World Tourism Organisation (UNWTO) promotes development of responsible, sustainable and universally accessible tourism. Companies have different strategies to make best use of environmental resources, for example hotel chains may encourage guests to reuse towels during their stays, so the hotel will use less water washing towels. They may reduce environmental damage, for example by limiting visitor numbers. They also respect local cultures and values by involving local people. Sustainability in tourism is partly a shared response from many industries to the dangers of global warming, but partly a way of maintaining tourist income into the future.

## SPOTLIGHT

### Water resources and tourism

Overuse of freshwater resources at tourist destinations in drier places leaves less water for locals. The biggest consumers of water are large hotels with ensuite bathrooms and pools, and the development of tourist amenities such as golf courses. In 2008 the local government of Phoenix, Arizona, approved plans to create a vast waterpark for tourists even though their reservoirs and groundwater resources were at their lowest levels for 11 years.

Creating a lush golf course in a desert diverts scarce water resources from other uses, yet attracts tourist income.

## Considering others

The arrival of tourists changes many cultural and social aspects of societies. The most beneficial global improvement is that both visitors and hosts learn more about, and gain respect for, the diversity of people, beliefs and opportunities in the world. In some places this can lead to improved education, healthcare and equality in society. For example, in places such as Costa Rica, where traditionally women do mostly domestic work, more women are getting jobs and income from the tourism industry. Social changes in LDCs are sometimes encouraged by visitors from MDCs, who pay for new facilities such as water storage tanks to help villages they have stayed in. The tourist industry can help to preserve cultures when tourists buy traditional handicrafts or pay to watch traditional dances.

A tourist poses for a photo with African people in traditional dress. One debate about tourism is whether the industry helps indigenous culture survive for its own sake, or whether it promotes the versions of cultures that tourists want to see.

## Local problems

The negative effects of visitors on societies are very varied. Tourism can create stratification in societies in terms of wealth. For example, in Cuba, taxi drivers and tour guides for tourists earn more than lawyers and doctors, so the legal and medical professions are less valued in society. In addition, behaviour that tourists consider acceptable may be offensive to other cultures. For example, women are generally expected to cover their bodies and behave modestly in Islamic countries, so female tourists wearing bikinis or holding hands with men can cause offence. Tourists may stimulate antisocial behaviour in local people. Excessive drinking and drug use amongst tourists can cause drink and drug problems amongst locals, who are often too poor to afford such habits and may turn to begging or theft.

## SPOTLIGHT

### Disappearing languages

The geographical variation in language is changing partly as a result of tourism. For example, fewer people are learning to speak Gaelic in the Isle of Skye, Scotland, since tourism became economically important on the island. About 96 per cent of the languages in the world are spoken by only 4 per cent of the world's population. English, Spanish and increasingly Chinese are by far the most globally widespread languages. People in the tourism industry who can trade with or offer services to tourists in these languages may get more business than those who cannot.

## Travels into the future

In future, the tourism industry will spread into exciting new destinations away from land, including space and the undersea world. For example, plans for Hydropolis promise a resort with 220 luxury suites, a ballroom, a spa, restaurants and shops, all on the seafloor of the Persian Gulf. The success of this novel project could stimulate underwater tourism in a variety of global ocean settings. This would require development of new underwater engineering techniques, whose success or failure will depend in part on their environmental impact.

Space may be the next tourist frontier, following the offer of flights to the edges of Earth's atmosphere by Virgin Galactic.

## Going green

Sustainable or green tourism is already a growing trend. As the 21st century unfolds, there will be greater regulation from governments towards responsible tourism, as oil reserves dwindle further and the effects of global warming increase. As virtual social networking in computer worlds is becoming more popular, will our travels also become increasingly virtual? Will there be high street travel agents in years to come, or could we experience holidays without actually leaving our living rooms?

**CASE STUDY UNCOVERED**

On 26th December 2004, a strong earthquake on the ocean floor west of Indonesia caused a massive tsunami. Waves slammed into coastlines all around the Indian Ocean, from Somalia to Malaysia. The tsunami hit during peak tourist season, when many visitors from MDCs were in the region for Christmas holidays. This was by far the biggest natural disaster on record, both in scale and impact, as it ruined the lives of millions of people. Reconstruction has happened fast, largely to rebuild the coastal tourism industry upon which parts of the region depend. However, this process has led to many problems for local people, who have been excluded from their homes and former lives by the tourism industry. Some people call this the second tsunami.

This map shows the areas worst affected by the 2004 tsunami, as well as the estimated number of deaths.

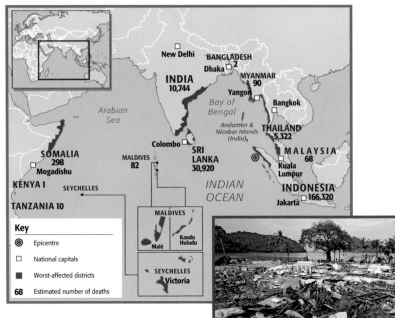

Thailand's Phi Phi Island resort looked like this (right) after the tsunami.

## Disaster and response

The tsunami waves killed 230,000 people, washed away whole beaches and villages, ruined infrastructure such as roads and bridges, and displaced millions. The disaster affected many coastal industries such as fishing, but tourism was one of the most visibly damaged. The spotlight of the Western media was turned on Thai resorts, where around 2,250 foreign holidaymakers died, even though many more local people died in Indonesia. The disaster had personal importance to many people in MDCs who knew the region from holidays or knew people personally affected.

A massive total sum of £4.7 billion in international aid was spent on the Indian Ocean tsunami. The greatest government donors included Australia and Germany, whose tour industries were significantly affected by the event, but in the UK donations from individuals exceeded government pledges. Thousands of troops, healthcare and charity workers and engineers descended on the region to help the injured, collect the dead and start the clear-up operation.

## Staying away

Many Western visitors in less-affected areas continued with their holidays, and some survivors stayed on to help the relief effort. However, many visitors cancelled holidays they had already booked. Some felt it was inappropriate to visit resorts such as Phuket in Thailand, where so many had died, while others were concerned about health risks and damage to infrastructure that might affect their travel plans. In the months following the tsunami, earnings for the thousands of businesses dependent on tourism plummeted. In Phuket, the number of hotel rooms occupied was about 15 per cent of normal levels, around 400 hotels, restaurants and tourist shops closed, and tourism businesses lost an estimated £1 billion. Foreign tourists even stayed away from areas where the tsunami did not strike, such as the Pacific coast of Thailand, because they thought from media images that all beaches in the country were out of action.

## SPOTLIGHT

### Economic impact on tourism

The table below gives data on the importance of the tourism industry for different countries impacted by the tsunami. Which country do you think was affected most?

|  | Sri Lanka | Thailand | Maldives |
|---|---|---|---|
| Tourism % total employment | 9 | 9 | 54 |
| Number of tourists in 2003 | 501,000 | 10,000,000 | 564,000 |
| Tourism earnings (% of 2005 GDP) | 5 | 5 | 42 |
| Number of tourism jobs affected by tsunami | 30,000 | 500,000 | 25,000 |
| Estimated damage to tourism (million £) | 168 | 670 | 200 |

### Bringing back the tourists

In the weeks after the tsunami, the tourist boards of Sri Lanka, Thailand and the Maldives urged foreign visitors to return immediately, so local people could quickly start to earn money from tourists. The regional tourism regulating body, PETA, and individual countries, started a drive to attract visitors by advertising and promoting the region. For example, the Thai government paid to host the high-profile Miss World competition in the tsunami-affected region.

At the same time, different governments in the affected countries made long-term plans to reduce the effects of any future tsunamis on the region. One way was to start to construct an ocean-wide tsunami warning system, to give people more chance of escape. Another was to implement laws to prevent building too close to the coast. The authorities established coastal regulation zones (in India) or conservation buffer zones (in Thailand and Burma), limiting the building or rebuilding of structures within 100 or 200 metres of the ocean edge.

### How tourism dependency affects local people

In many Indian Ocean regions, businesspeople in charge of coastal recovery handed over power to redevelopers, some of whom worked directly for the tourism industry. Many homeless locals had to stay in relief camps, patrolled by soldiers and dependent on aid. Redevelopers rebuilt tourist hotels on cleared beaches, sometimes within buffer zones, but built new settlements for former coastal fishing

Rapid clear-up of beaches and reconstruction of tourist infrastructure continued while visitors soaked up the sun.

communities many kilometres inland. This made it virtually impossible for local people to transport nets or engines to their boats and run fishing businesses. Access was made worse because developers 'privatised' beachfront land by putting up fences, employing security guards and building private roads. By the end of 2005, most of the resort islands of the Maldives had reopened for normal business, but 90,000 local people on other, non-tourist islands were still short of drinkable water.

Those still living near the coast were increasingly squeezed out by the region's economic dependency on tourism. Vulnerable survivors with little business experience were offered less money for their beachside land than it was really worth. Former fishermen were excluded from all but the most poorly paid jobs in the new tourism ventures as they lacked experience. Many workers were exploited by the industry. For example, in one case Burmese workers in Thailand building hotels were not paid for six months of labour and were beaten when they asked for the money.

## PERSPECTIVES FOR DEBATE

"In a cruel twist of fate, nature has presented Sri Lanka with an unique opportunity, and out of this great tragedy will come a world class tourism destination."

Sri Lanka Tourist Board, 2005

"It is vital to follow the non-negotiable principle of not further victimising the victims of the tsunami. It is very important to safeguard against any moves to convert the disaster into an opportunity to displace the local communities living along the coast."

United Nations Recovery Team, Frontline, April/May 2005

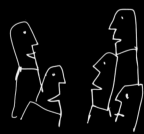

## Tsunami and the environment

The tsunami affected coastal land in different ways. In some places, beaches were protected from the waves by natural features such as headlands. In others, human processes such as the removal of coral reefs, mangroves and sand dunes, to make way for shipping and seaside buildings, exposed the coast to severe harm. The Surin Islands of Thailand were among the least damaged places in the region as their reefs were intact. But the waves also destroyed 30 per cent of Indonesia's coral reefs. The biggest and longest-term effect on the region's environment came with the large volumes of seawater that entered freshwater wells and soaked into farmland. This has reduced the amount of fresh water and farmed food available for both tourists and local people.

# SPOTLIGHT

### Greedy tourism

The large quantities of tsunami reconstruction funds proved too tempting for some regional groups in tourism. Almost £10 million from the Government of India's Tsunami Rehabilitation Programme was allocated to Kerala Tourism for 'beach beautification'. This involved 20 projects in areas that were not even affected by the disaster. Local communities complained about this misuse of funds that could have helped them to rebuild their fishing industries. Kerala Tourism rebranded the schemes as 'coastal protection', even though they included such items as flowerpots, lampposts and an amphitheatre! Kerala Tourism says that attracting tourists will provide work for locals, but locals say they should have been consulted. What do you think?

## Indian Ocean tourism today

The tsunami depressed tourism and income in many countries, such as Thailand where tourist arrivals were down 40 per cent even two years after the disaster. The recovery of tourism has also been interrupted by other events, such as civil war in Sri Lanka in 2006 and the closure of major Thai airports in late 2008 during political turmoil. In places such as the Maldives, tourist volume is now greater than it was in 2004. In Indonesia too, coral reefs that attract dive tourists may be recovering quicker than anticipated by experts, as with a smaller coastal fishing industry there is less destructive fishing on the reefs. Nevertheless, normal life has not recovered for many local populations affected by the tsunami. There are still around 10,000 Sri Lankans displaced by the waters, still living in temporary camps.

## Sustainable future?

Some recovered parts of the region have promoted sustainable tourism businesses in an attempt to maintain long-term tourism income with minimal environmental impact. In 2008, the new USAID-funded Arugam Bay bridge in south-eastern Sri Lanka opened. This links coastal towns such as Pottuvil with the mainland, allowing easy and quick access to the bay from airports. In 2007, Arugam received the Best Destination award at the World Travel Market World Responsible Tourism Awards. This prestigious award is given to a destination that is making a significant commitment to the culture and economies of local communities and to biodiversity conservation. There is a new community eco-guide association in Arugam, training local guides to lead tours that promote environmental care, and also investment in accommodation in the form of locals' homes and small guesthouses.

This double photo shows views of Banda Aceh, Indonesia, soon after the tsunami (top) and almost a year later (bottom). This town is on the closest landmass to the tsunami's epicentre.

The range of tourism opportunities in South Africa today is largely the result of a deliberate government drive to become part of the globalised tourism industry. The government has tried to achieve this through involving a far broader cross-section of South Africans in the industry than was possible in the past.

## A new beginning

The numbers of foreign tourists visiting South Africa was consistently low until the end of apartheid in 1990. Many people stayed away out of protest against this system of limiting civil rights for black South Africans. Then, in 1994, a new government led by Nelson Mandela embarked on a Reconstruction and Development Programme (RDP) to improve conditions for the largely poor population and to build the economy. Increasing sustainable tourism was quickly identified as an ideal way to push ahead the RDP.

Post-apartheid, there was an increased flow of tourists to South Africa. Many of them came from the UK, Germany and the Netherlands, which were all former colonial powers in southern Africa. Many businesses in the global tourism industry saw the potential for selling holidays in the new South Africa and attracting visitors from all over the world. For Europeans, South Africa offered a warm climate just a few hours away by modern aeroplane, and in the same time zone, so visitors would not suffer jet-lag. In addition, the country had the best roads and rail network in Africa. Travel companies and other tourism businesses in MDCs started to invest in South Africa. Airlines set up new services from MDCs to South Africa, such as USAfrica Airways' flights from Washington to Johannesburg that began in 1994.

## SPOTLIGHT

### Early tourism

South African tourism began with wildlife. The first South African national park, the Kruger, was created to protect wildlife from hunting and opened to rich international visitors in 1927. Cheaper flights in the 1960s increased numbers of European tourists, but global opposition to apartheid in the 1970s and 1980s slowed the industry once more.

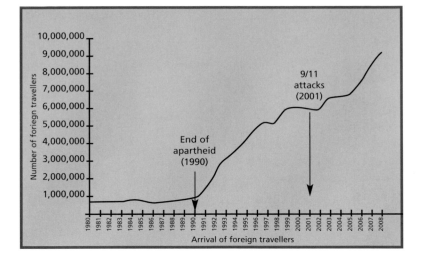

End of apartheid (1990)

9/11 attacks (2001)

Arrival of foreign travellers

Tourist arrivals have increased in response to changing political trends in South Africa, but also dipped during the global dent in travel confidence following the terrorist attacks of 9/11 in the USA.

## Diversification

Up until the 1990s, most tourists from MDCs came to South Africa to visit the 16 national parks, concentrated in the Northern Cape region. The South African government was aware of the rich potential for diversifying tourism in the country, given the variety of its attractions. Diversifying the tourist industry meant increasing the destinations and types of holidays offered to tourists. This in turn increased the participation of locals in the tourism industry.

South Africa Tourism, the official government agency, tried to attract more visitors to different parts of the country, from the Drakensberg Mountains and the beaches of Durban, to vibrant modern cities such as Cape Town. In one marketing exercise they repainted 50 London taxis in the colours of the South African flag and flew the British cab drivers to South Africa so they could chat about the country with their passengers back in London. They also made use of the growing global internet to advertise new travel options.

South Africa's diverse habitats range from high mountains and grassland to desert and coast.

### Changing the scale and breadth of tourism

The South African government focused on small-scale diversification in a wide range of areas. It supported small- to medium-sized enterprises run by local people, rather than large tourism operators. Those who have benefited include operators of small guesthouses, bars and restaurants that provide local cuisine, people offering community tours or traditional music, arts and crafts, and support services such as transportation and laundry.

## SPOTLIGHT

#### Sho't Left

The South African Department of Environmental Affairs and Tourism (DEAT) runs a programme called Sho't Left, which means 'get off at the next corner'. This programme encourages South Africans to travel more within their own country by providing them with information about tourist attractions as well as access to tour operators offering reasonably priced tour packages. International tourism is vital for the industry's growth, but domestic tourism within South Africa is also important. In 2006, South African residents took 37 million internal trips and 29 million of these were to see family and friends. The challenge is to change the domestic tourism market from one that is driven by the need to visit family or friends to one that is driven by family or individual lifestyle choices.

South Africa's unique flora is one of its diverse attractions for the tourism industry.

The government designated more national parks from 1994 onwards, making a current total of 20, and also helped to create over 9,000 small reserves by making nationally owned former grazing and farmland available to private owners. The reserves provide a diverse range of opportunities for tourists to see wildlife at differing scales of luxury.

There have also been new trends in South African tourism, such as shark encounters and historical or heritage tourism. Many global visitors now flock to see sights significant to the apartheid years, such as Robben Island, the former prison where Mandela was detained by the South African government. To make sure that the tourism industry continues into the future, South Africa introduced Travel and Tourism courses in all secondary schools in the country from 2000 onwards.

## New tourist sector

South Africa is one of the pioneering countries in promoting fair trade tourism. The organisation Fair Trade in Tourism South Africa (FTTSA), set up in 2004, analyses tour operators on different criteria, such as whether the company offers fair wages and good working conditions, involvement in decision-making by staff, ethical business practice and respect for human rights, culture and the environment. For example, they score companies on whether they favour employing people who are historically disadvantaged in South African tourism, including black, female or disabled people. They issue fair trade certificates and offer support to businesses that meet these criteria. At the end of 2008, the 40 certificate holders ranged from whole nature reserves and exclusive wilderness lodges to backpacker lodges and even bicycle tours in a poor township. The FTTSA website is a globally recognised resource about sustainable tourism that attracts 300,000 hits each month. Many tourism organisations establish web links with the site each year.

Tourists taking fair trade township tours in Cape Town transport their local guides with them as they go.

## The effects of tourism governance

Between 1994 and 2008, as a result of the promotion and regulation of tourism by the South African government, the number of foreign tourists arriving in South Africa grew from 3.7 million to 9 million. About half of all visitors are from European countries and the USA, but the biggest increases have been in visitors from Asia and other parts of Africa. The South African tourism industry employs over 1 million people and contributes over 8 per cent of total GDP, a higher percentage than the gold-mining industry, which was the highest-earning sector for decades.

Many South African tourism companies continue to use new technology to promote their global business. For example, KwaZulu province has installed web cams to allow viewers of their website to see the kinds of wildlife they might experience on a real safari. Southern Africa Direct is a UK television channel that promotes South Africa to the 9 million subscribers of Sky TV.

Tourism has triggered social and economic development in previously impoverished areas such as townships. Some of this is quite small scale. For example, in the poor suburb of New Brighton, near Port Elizabeth, tourists with Calabash Tours take a break for refreshments at the Charles Duna Primary School. The money they pay is used to run the school in the absence of sufficient government funding.

This diagram shows some of the links between the local economy and tourism that are strengthened by fair trade and sustainable tourism. Many of these links are affected when tourism is dominated by TNCs.

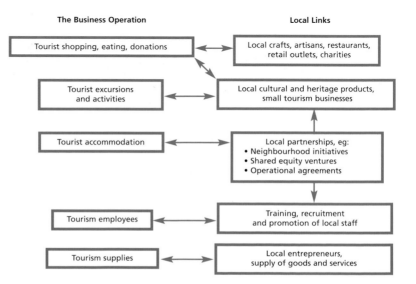

## Problems in the industry

The spread of tourism is not without problems. Some tourist hotels, like businesses in other South African industries such as construction or agriculture, employ migrant workers who don't expect to be paid as much as South Africans. This has fuelled tension amongst poor locals against immigrants. As in many LDCs, the presence of rich tourists has also been a focus for crime. Criminal acts have ranged from petty theft and muggings to murders, especially in Johannesburg. Publicity about the crimes in MDCs has caused tourists to cancel bookings, even to safer areas of the country.

The South African government estimates that one job is created for every 12 foreign arrivals, yet some other LDCs claim a ratio of one for every eight visitors. The challenges for South Africa are to change this ratio by developing better tourist infrastructure, encouraging more tourists and making them spend more at the tourist attractions across the country. South African tourism was given a boost when the country hosted the soccer World Cup in 2010 and saw an influx of more than 300,000 visitors to the tournament.

Students study ecotourism at a college developed by the owners of the Grootbos Private Nature Reserve, South Africa. Projects like this aim to boost the country's tourist income in a sustainable way for the future.

CASE STUDY UNCOVERED

Accor is a dominant TNC in the tourism industry. Its chain of hotels cater to a wide range of tastes and budgets, from the inexpensive, such as F1 or Ibis hotels, to the luxurious, such as the Sofitel. Like many other companies, Accor's business has expanded partly as a result of the global spread of new technology, including the rise in bookings via the internet.

## History of Accor

The Accor group started in 1967, when Gérard Pelisson and Paul Dubrule spotted a gap in the market for US-style motels in Europe. Their plan was to offer standardised rooms, good parking, and restaurants with local food, close to major roads. They opened the first Novotel in Lille, France, and then expanded by taking over the Mercure, Ibis and Sofitel hotel groups in Europe during the late 1970s. The company was renamed Accor in 1983 and through the 1990s and 2000s expanded into the USA and Asia. In 2008, the Accor group ran 4,000 hotels – more than any other tourism TNC. It operated mostly in Europe, and was growing at a rate of 40,000 rooms per year. The group's headquarters has always been in Evry, France, which was the founders' home town.

## Travel goes online

The world wide web has had a massive impact on the travel industry in recent years. In the USA alone, online travel booking doubled between 2003 and 2008. Travel tickets and accommodation are the most-purchased items over the internet in many countries. About one-third of all trips by American tourists are booked online, and most of these are through travel agents such as ebookers, Lastminute.com and Expedia. Like high street travel agents, these companies get paid by companies such as hotel groups and airlines for booking clients through their sites. However, web prices are often cheaper as they do not have many staff or overheads such as premises to pay for. Other benefits of travel websites include the ease of comparing what is included in holidays, and also help in finding specialist or individualised holidays.

Accor launched its first website, Accorhotels.com, in 2000. This offered details about its different hotels, links to information about the places where the hotels were, and an online booking service. It received about 12 million hits during the first year, and customers booked 1 million rooms online. By 2003, the number of online bookings had risen more than four-fold.

## SPOTLIGHT

### The globalisation of Accor

1967 The first Novotel opens in Lille, France.

1973 Coventry Novotel, the first in the UK, is opened.

1974 The first Ibis hotel (economy brand) opens in Bordeaux, France.

1975 The company acquires Mercure (midscale brand).

1980 The group buys Sofitel (luxury brand).

1983 Novotel group becomes Accor.

1985 Accor creates the Formule 1 (F1) no-frills budget room concept.

1987 The group diversifies into restaurant vouchers for employees and care homes for the elderly.

1990 Accor buys Motel 6, a budget chain in the USA.

1991 The company acquires Compagnie International des Wagons-Lits et du Tourism, including the Etap hotel chain, on-board train services and highway restaurants.

1999 Accor buys Red Roof Inns in the USA.

2000 Accorhotels.com is launched.

2001 The group expands into China.

2002 Accor buys a 30 per cent stake in the German hotel company Dorint AG and opens the first Sofitel in the UK.

2004 A one-third stake is bought in Groupe Lucien Barriere, a European casino group.

2005 Accor opens its 4,000th hotel.

2007 The group launches the Pullman chain of upscale business hotels.

This map shows the number of Accor hotels in various world locations in December 2011.

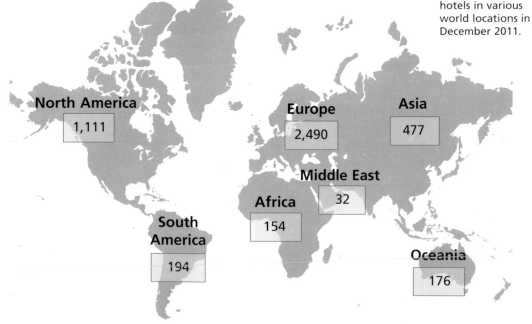

North America
1,111

Europe
2,490

Asia
477

Middle East
32

Africa
154

South America
194

Oceania
176

### Website changes

By 2004, Accor got 8 per cent of its sales revenue from online bookings, but discovered that the costs of these bookings were much higher than expected. The reason was that there were several website intermediaries, such as search engines and travel agents, to whom Accor paid a commission to bring in customers. Some of these sites offered Accor's rooms more cheaply than the group's own website. Accor therefore decided to change how it paid its intermediaries, in particular by varying commissions. Less effort was needed to market rooms in high tourism seasons, such as summer, so Accor paid intermediaries less at this time. Intermediaries were paid more in low seasons because they were bringing in trade during quiet patches. Managers of individual hotels controlled the varying commissions via the centralised Accor IT system. Accor started emailing people who had previously booked online with details of hotel promotions and information about the group, in order to retain and repeat their custom.

### Economies of scale

Large global hotel chains have many advantages over independent hotels in what are known as economies of scale. Individual hotels in the chain have use of a centralised IT system and website, pre-existing marketing strategies and branding such as hotel logos or upholstery colours, and even shared management staff between different hotels. This can reduce costs to a hotel considerably. It is generally cheaper to build and furnish several hotels to the same design. For example, F1 motels are built using prefabricated panels, forming identically sized rooms. Hotel chains can also buy commodities, such as bed linen, toilet paper and televisions, in bulk to keep costs down.

When travellers stop at any Motel 6 across North America, they know what standards to expect in this inexpensive Accor brand of roadside accommodation.

## Financial strategies

Accor has a changing strategy about its biggest costs: buying hotels or land to build them on. With rising property prices in the 21st century, Accor started to sell off many hotels to new owners, who took on Accor-trained management and kept the Accor brand.

Accor also opened new Accor-branded hotels without actually paying for their development. Between 2003 and 2008, the group opened 113,000 rooms, which cost over £5 billion, but only directly invested £400 million. The rest came from financial investors keen to buy into the successful brand. Maintaining the name and standards, while cutting costs and expanding worldwide, especially into growing markets such as Asia, is helping Accor to thrive in the competitive global tourism industry.

## SPOTLIGHT

### Corporate responsibility

Accor has different corporate initiatives to reduce its negative impacts. Each year, the Accor group uses as much energy as a city of 350,000 people. It is trying to reduce this consumption, for example by fitting solar water heaters on 100 new French hotels. It has also introduced carbon neutral conferencing at Mercure hotels, where it matches the cost of greenhouse emissions produced during conferences to pay for emission-reduction schemes. Accor assists local communities by displaying the work of young artists in hotels and works with NGOs to prevent sex tourism in its Asian hotels.

The once independent Old Cataract Hotel, Aswan, on the Nile in Egypt, is now a Sofitel.

**CASE STUDY UNCOVERED**

Uluru, formerly known as Ayers Rock, is a symbol of the natural beauty and spiritual draw of the desert area in central Australia. It is therefore an icon of the global tourist industry. Thousands of visitors experience the rock each year, many to climb to the top, and their visits bring positive economic impacts to both tourism companies and the indigenous people in the area, the Aborigines. The climbing tourists bring negative cultural and environmental impacts, including the wearing away of the rock itself. Balancing these impacts of global tourism is critical in the future development of this site.

Uluru stands out from the Australian desert as a tourist lure, with Uluru-Kata Tjuta Cultural Centre in the foreground.

## The lifecycle of tourism

Look at any popular tourist destination and it is difficult to imagine it without visitors. Over time, the number of visitors a place attracts grows slowly, then much faster, and finally reaches a steady level. The level depends on many factors, such as the volume of people that an area can accommodate and the local infrastructure. Sometimes the number of visitors has a negative impact on the destination. For example, if a small campsite in the Rockies, USA, becomes too popular, the extra litter and noise may put off further campers. At luxury Caribbean resorts, tourist numbers are strictly limited to keep them quiet and exclusive. When tourist development is carried out carefully, or attractions are added, visitor numbers may increase. For example, the coastal resort of Atlantic City, USA, lost visitors after people chose to holiday elsewhere, but rejuvenated tourism by encouraging gambling casinos.

## Ups and downs at Uluru

At Uluru, the lifecycle of tourism began in the 1940s with the first tracks leading to the remote site from roads crossing central Australia. During the 1950s, tours from nearby Alice Springs started, and motels, an airstrip and other infrastructure were established as reports of the beautiful rock spread amongst visitors to Australia. There were a few thousand tourists each year. Infrastructure for tourism developed over the following decades and visitor numbers rose.

Owing to litter and other problems associated with visitors, camps and motels next to Uluru were closed in the 1980s and a resort 15 kilometres from Uluru called Yulara was developed for tourists. The rate of visitors to Uluru has grown steadily, particularly after the rock was made a World Heritage Site in 1987 for its natural beauty. By 2008, there were over 400,000 visitors to Uluru each year.

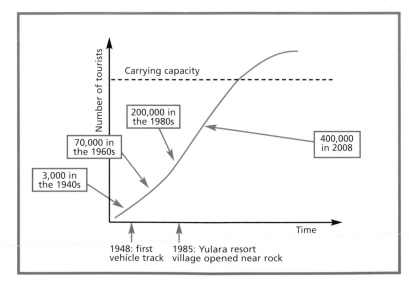

This graph shows the rise in tourist numbers at Uluru from the 1940s to 2008, with the predicted rise into the future. As with any other tourist destination, Uluru's carrying capacity is the number of visitors it can take without damaging or spoiling the site.

## Cultural importance

Uluru is more than just a beautiful, red sandstone mountain in the middle of desert lands. It is also incredibly important to the cultural life of the Anangu. The Anangu, made up of the Pitjantjatjara and Yankuntjatjara ethnic groups, have lived in the Uluru region for about 40,000 years. They have ancestral stories where creator beings, in the form of plants, animals and people, forged the landscape of Australia, and Uluru is especially sacred as home to spirits of some of the creator beings. The Anangu believe that the folded shape of the rock is a monument to ancient spirit wars and that the rock is criss-crossed with spirit routes. Living close to and preserving Uluru is important to Anangu people as part of their traditional law and culture, called tjukurpa. Under tjukurpa, the Anangu make some areas around Uluru out of bounds for non-Aborigines. Climbing the rock is very rare in Anangu society. It is only ever undertaken by a few men on special occasions.

Hand markings and drawings on rocks around Uluru are testament to its spiritual and cultural significance to the Anangu.

## The climb

About half of all visitors to Uluru climb the 1.6 kilometres to the top of the rock, often to see sunrise or sunset. The Anangu discourage visitors from climbing the rock for two reasons. The first is tjukurpa and the second is safety. Over the years, more than 30 visitors have died on the rock, usually following falls related to heat exhaustion, and the traditional owners feel responsibility for these accidents.

The Anangu provide information about the sacred nature of the rock via a cultural centre, information signs, leaflets and through official tour guides. When tourists buy visitor permits to get up close to the rock, guides actively promote walking around the base, a trip of 9.4 kilometres incorporating caves and Aboriginal rock art, rather than climbing it. However, many tourists arriving at Uluru have no idea about the cultural importance of the site and indeed see the climb as the major activity once they have arrived. Interestingly, European tourists are the least likely to climb Uluru after learning about Anangu culture, and Australians and Japanese are the most likely.

Uluru is important for drawing visitors to the Australian interior from the numerous popular coastal destinations.

## SPOTLIGHT

### Why people visit Uluru

In 2001, Northern Territory Tourism undertook a survey of international visitors where they asked people what motivated them to visit the region. Here are the top seven results of the survey:

| 1 | To see icons including Uluru | 70 per cent |
|---|---|---|
| 2 | To see the outback/wilderness | 61 per cent |
| 3 | To go somewhere different | 45 per cent |
| 4 | To see wildlife in a natural setting | 37 per cent |
| 5 | To explore or have an adventure | 34 per cent |
| 6 | To experience real Aboriginal culture | 33 per cent |
| 7 | To visit World Heritage sites | 30 per cent |

What do these results tell you about attitudes to the cultural significance of Uluru?

## Erosion and other growing impacts

The continued presence of tourists on Uluru is gradually increasing environmental damage. The major effect is erosion of the sandstone rock by walkers. An Uluru park ranger estimates that for every 100 tourists who climb the rock, 100 years-worth of damage is done to its surface. In peak tourist season there are as many as 7,000 visitors to Uluru each day. Their feet are slowly wearing away the rock, and some tourists even remove chunks of rock from Uluru as souvenirs. The co-managers of Uluru restrict erosion by keeping visitors to single paths and have installed chain rails to help tourists climb the rock. But the tourism industry also has a variety of impacts at ground level. Visitors trample plants around the rock and disturb wildlife, erode soil and sometimes accidentally start bush fires.

Many people think the levels of tourism at Uluru are beginning to exceed their environmental, cultural and economic carrying capacities.

## Benefit to Anangu

Why don't the Anangu ban climbing? One reason is that their ownership arrangement with the Australian government does not allow it. But the other is that, even though tolerating climbing does not fit with tjukurpa, tourists bring regular income and employment to the local Anangu community. Their income includes the payment of an annual rent (AU$150,000 in 1999) by the government and a 25 per cent share of gate receipts, which amounted to AU$1,750,000 in 2000. Mass tourism poses a threat to the Anangu, but also keeps their culture alive through educating non-Aborigines.

In future, the Anangu may get greater income from and control over tourism at Uluru. In October 2008, the large GPT property group put the Ayers Rock Resort at Yulara up for sale for AU$440 million. The Anangu people hope to purchase the hotel and restaurant resort once they can find investors, many of whom are affected by global financial problems. Uluru was on a shortlist for a global 2011 competition to become one of seven new wonders of nature. This publicity could stimulate greater numbers of global visitors, and climbers, and put greater pressure on the sustainability of Uluru tourism.

By taking more control of Uluru tourism, Anangu people hope to find the right balance between encouraging visitors and protecting their heritage.

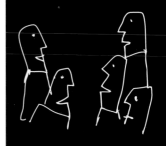

# Becoming an active global citizen

What is an active global citizen? It is someone who tries, in their own small way, to make the world a better place. To become an active global citizen, you will need to get involved in decisions that others make about your life and the lives of others around the world. Consider how the world could be changed, such as improving the environment, political or social conditions for others, and seek information about the issues from a wide variety of sources. Then go public by presenting your arguments to others, from classmates and local groups to national politicians and global organisations.

## In your life

Hopefully this book has prompted you to think about how your actions as a tourist affect the rest of the planet. The tourism industry is massive, with complex interdependencies between people, cultures and nations. So how can you get involved in tourism issues and maybe even help to make the global tourism industry more sustainable?

**Chart your travels**. A good way to start becoming an active global citizen is to consider your own and your family's impact through tourism. Where have you been on holiday in your life? Use maps and atlases to work out the distances you have travelled. How did you get there and what tourism services did you use? Did you learn the language or about the culture before you left? Did you use travel companies owned and run by locals or by TNCs? What has been your total environmental impact? For a long-distance flight, average carbon emissions are 120g per kilometre. There are lots of carbon calculators on the internet that you can use to check your impact. How could you have lessened any negative impacts or enjoyed your trips more?

**The industry at home.** How does tourism affect the place where you live? Consider the reasons why visitors come. What are the different businesses, services and facilities making up the tourist industry locally? What would you do to improve local tourism, make it more sustainable, involve more locals and encourage more travellers?

**Wake up to the world around you.** We are all exposed to masses of tourism information, ranging from travel programmes and adverts on television to travel photos of relatives and friends, to magazine and newspaper articles. A lot of information is presented simply to tempt people to visit places and spend money there, and rarely lays out the issues of travel in that destination. Scratch away at the surface of what the industry wants you to see and investigate what lies beneath. Use your awareness of the interconnectedness of tourism with other industries to discover the real impacts of travellers in different global destinations now and into the future.

## Key terms for internet searches

Type these terms into a search engine on the internet and see what results you get. How many hits appear? Are the websites from around the world, and are there any sources that surprise you?

Travel agent
World Tourism Organisation
Ethical travel
Tourism Concern
Fair trade in tourism
Women in tourism
Globalisation and tourism
Travel hotspot
Cultural impacts of travel
Tourism statistics

International hotel group
Pros and cons of tourism
Different types of tourism, eg:
• adventure tourism
• ecotourism or green tourism
• medical tourism
• poorism
• sex tourism
• shock tourism
• tombstone tourism

## Data watch

Keep on top of global statistics by visiting these thought-provoking websites.

### www.worldmapper.org
The difference with the maps on this site is that countries and regions are distorted according to the data they represent. Here are a few interesting maps to explore: 19) Tourism destinations; 20) Tourist origins; 28) Aircraft flights; 154) Living on up to $10; and 158) Living on over $200.

### www.worldometers.info
Have you ever wanted to see the rate at which data such as world population, energy use or the number of computers sold change? Then check out this website for up-to-the-minute information.

### www.peopleandplanet.net
This is a fascinating place to explore different aspects of the interdependencies between people and our world, and sustainability. Click on the 'Eco Tourism' link on the left of the opening page to get to the tourism section. At the top of that page there are links to a newsfile for media stories on tourism, links to other websites and recommended books, and interesting factfiles. These contain up-to-date information about many aspects of the global tourism industry and its impacts, such as child labour in tourism, the importance of women as tourism workers, and the rise in cruise tourism.

# Topic web

Use this topic web to discover the themes and ideas in subject areas related to the tourism industry.

## Geography

Investigate the monsoon in India by examining climographs for different regions of India, using the internet or atlases. How does the monsoon affect tourism in different states of India? What types of generic holiday would you expect to find in different areas of the country?

## Citizenship

Exploitation can be a feature of the tourism industry. What tourism destinations should you stay away from because local people are being exploited? Visit the Tourism Concern website (www.tourismconcern.org.uk) to find out more. Weigh up the pros and cons of your staying away for local people who are reliant on tourism.

## English

Create the script for a podcast that would guide a teenage tourist on a walking route around a tourist destination. Use persuasive and descriptive language to point out interesting sites and to keep the tourist's interest.

## Maths

Search for 'tourism' at http://data.un.org/Data.aspx to locate data on international tourism expenditure. Select 20 data, by region, by LDC or MDC, or at random to collect a wide range of values. Create a bar chart to show global differences in spending. Is it fair to draw conclusions from these data alone?

## The Tourism Industry

## Science

Find out how coral reefs form, and about the environmental conditions they need to thrive. What effect is global warming having on oceans and reefs? How is coastal tourism having positive and negative effects on this ecosystem?

## ICT

Create a Powerpoint presentation for a new sustainable tourism operator. You should create a master slide with a logo, a main title and a main menu linking to subsequent slides. The next slides should each offer a different type of accommodation, excursion or other aspect of the company. Include your own pictures or those you download from the Internet.

## History

Research colonial centres of the past that remain important tourism destinations of today. What makes them important or interesting?

# Glossary

**biodiversity** The range of plants and animals, and the habitat in which they live, used as a measure of biological health in a region.

**brand** A symbol, mark or quality that characterises a product. It has been called 'a product's personality'.

**buffer zone** An area created to keep two other areas separate for some reason, such as danger from wave damage.

**commission** A fee for services undertaken, based on a percentage of the amount received or agreed to be paid.

**composite** Made up of many separate parts.

**culture** Accumulated habits, attitudes, languages, customs and beliefs of a group of people that define their general behaviour and way of life.

**diversification** Establishing new products and markets, sometimes outside normal areas of business, to increase sales.

**erosion** The carrying away of a worn-down substance such as rock or soil.

**GDP (gross domestic product)** The value of all goods and services produced by a country in a single year.

**global warming** The average global temperature rise that most scientists agree is caused by increases in greenhouse gases such as carbon dioxide, released largely by human machines, in the atmosphere.

**governance** The way an organisation is run and controlled politically, economically and administratively.

**greenhouse gases** Atmospheric gases, such as carbon dioxide and water vapour, that contribute to the greenhouse effect that is warming the planet.

**green tourism** Using and providing tourist services that are sustainable, with especially low resource use, for example by conserving water and power.

**heritage tourism** Visiting and providing tourist services at locations with sites or monuments that are significant to regional or national culture.

**infrastructure** The systems that support a country such as roads, water supply, waste, power supply, access to shops, and other resources.

**interdependent** When organisations, industries or individuals are mutually dependent on each other to make something work.

**International Monetary Fund (IMF)** An organisation that promotes global trade and economic stability by over-seeing financial arrangements between countries.

**less developed countries (LDCs)** Countries that have a lower income and poorer standards in health, nutrition, education and industry than more developed countries (MDCs).

**lobby** To attempt to influence or persuade others about changes to laws.

**medical tourism** When people travel for medical treatment or the opportunity to buy cheaper pharmaceutical products.

**more developed countries (MDCs)** Countries that have a higher income and better standards in health, nutrition, education and industry than less developed countries.

**motel** A building or group of buildings to accommodate travellers by road, often with parking spaces by the rooms.

**national park** A reserve of public land, usually owned and controlled by a government, to protect animals and plants that live there.

**resort** A place developed for leisure, often in a tourist destination, usually providing accommodation, food and other services in one place.

**restoration** Returning something to its former state, prior to damage or change, usually as part of preservation of cultural heritage.

**sex tourism** Visiting a place in order to pay for sexual activity with residents there. Many sex tourists exploit poor or under-age individuals who are forced into prostitution.

**stratification** Identifying or establishing different layers, ranks or grades of a commodity.

**sustainable** Able to be maintained at a steady level for a long time, without causing environmental or social damage.

**transnational company (TNC)** A company that operates across several nations.

**tsunami** A series of waves caused by displacement of water following an earthquake beneath the ocean floor.

**World Bank** An international organisation that promotes economic development in the world's poorer nations.

# Index

# Global Industries Uncovered

## Contents of titles in the series:

WAYLAND